William Leonard Gage

Favorite Hymns in Their Original Form

William Leonard Gage

Favorite Hymns in Their Original Form

ISBN/EAN: 9783337083717

Printed in Europe, USA, Canada, Australia, Japan

Cover: Foto ©Thomas Meinert / pixelio.de

More available books at **www.hansebooks.com**

FAVORITE HYMNS

IN THEIR

ORIGINAL FORM.

SELECTED AND VERIFIED

BY

WILLIAM LEONARD GAGE.

———o———

NEW YORK:
A. S. BARNES & Co.,
1874.

TO MY BRETHREN

OF THE MINISTRY

IN HARTFORD,

THIS LITTLE BOOK IS INSCRIBED

IN TOKEN OF WARM LOVE AND

HEARTY ADMIRATION.

PREFACE.

This book has been born out of my own curiosity. Knowing that in all our modern hymn books we have many hymns rearranged, modified, or abridged, I desired to know for my own satisfaction, just how far these changes extend, and whether they are mutilations or improvements. The result has been a careful examination of hymns, and the bringing together in their original dress of those which I believe to be the chief favorites of American Christians. There are many others which are no less dear than those within these pages, but which find no place here, because they have been spared the touch of critics and hymn book compilers. Such, for example, are "Salvation! O the joyful sound:" "Come, Holy Spirit, heavenly Dove:"* "My God, the Spring

---

*I am convinced that the reading of the lines
"Dear Lord and shall we ever lie
At this poor dying rate."
was a misprint in the early English editions of Watts, and should be charged to live, not as an improvement but as the correction of a typographical error.

of all my joys:" "O for a closer walk with God:" "God moves in a mysterious way:" "Nearer my God to Thee." These may have been changed; but I have not met them other than their writers left them. Of the same general class of hymns are such as I have chosen: those which are known as widely as the English language is spoken. There are certain things which have come to us invested with associations so rich and tender, that we do not ask whether they are in themselves beautiful: their meaning to us is beauty enough. And these hymns are of them: for while some of them are perhaps lacking in the highest graces of expression, and are possibly a little hard and mechanical, they have been bathed in the great wave of Christian feeling and have come out therefrom sacred. They are, next to the Bible, the most precious possession of the church. I am not sure but they are the most precious possession of our language. It is a question which the Christian would not like to see decided against him, which were the harder to lose from our literature, the writings of Shakespeare or those hymns which have fed the hope and inspired the faith of so many generations of saints.

The really great and noble hymns are few. It

would surprise one not used to the task, to turn over the hundreds of the verses of Watts and Doddridge, and the Wesleys, and see how small is the residue which the world will not willingly let die. Those strains which pass the ordeal provided by one of the Church fathers as the test of sound doctrine, " what is accepted everywhere, at all times and by every one," would limit our hymnology to very narrow bounds. Few of our writers have produced more than a half-dozen really superior hymns: indeed, with the exception of Watts and Doddridge, and possibly of Charles Wesley, none have done so. Our choicest Christian spirits have economized this gift with rare thrift; and have condensed their wealth into most portable and accessible vessels. And this is the more strange when we remember that almost all celebrated hymns, as well as those not celebrated, have been thrown off in a heat: many of them by Christian ministers at the close of a sermon. They were not thought of as having any special worthiness: and doubtless their writers would be more amazed than we, could they now see, that all the world is singing what came to them in some gush of feeling, and dropped molten from their pens.

The test of this will be found in the crude

forms of many of these hymns. And I hope this little book will do for others what it has done for me, in reconciling the reader to the changes which modern taste has made in well-known hymns. It is the fashion of some to decry the custom of "doctoring" our standard hymns; yet I cannot doubt that he who examines this book, while glad to have in accessible form the original of many strains that he loves, will have little desire to go back to the old form.

The simple fact is that our older English hymn writers did not possess that trained ear for rhythm which is a distinguishing mark of our time. In Germany, Schiller and Goethe introduced a new era in melodious versification: and their contemporaries in England did a similar service to English poetry: and now the advance in this direction has become so great that it would seem impossible for language to be a more dainty and exquisite medium of melodious sound than it is in the hands of Tennyson and Longfellow. Such men as Doddridge and Watts had no such training: their lines seem harsh in this age of perfect versification: and there are many men whose tact and taste are so nicely cultivated that they can add to the graces of those hastily written hymns which men like Watts and Doddridge dashed off at the close of a sermon.

Besides, we have advanced to a time when the old would be the new: I mean, that the changes which have been made, have become a part of our life, and to bring back the original form would itself produce a shock to the sense of devoutness. To take up the line in Toplady's Rock of Ages: "When my eyestrings break in death," and attempt to bring it back instead of "When my eyelids close in death," would of course produce a painful sense of novelty. True, the original is far stronger and finer: it is poetry, while the modernized version is prose; flat and unsuggestive: an instance of change which has been no improvement. But the change has been made: and as the hymn books copy mainly from one another, the forms in which they are current has become tantamount to the original.

I have brought into this selection some hymns where the changes have been very slight, and yet are interesting. Such for instance is Heber's Missionary Hymn, where the words Ceylon's isle, were originally Java's isle. A larger class are those where I have given the whole hymn: that which we sing, not being greatly changed, but taken out of its connection and unity, and largely reduced in length.

I have no doubt that some persons, were they engaged on this task, would have greatly extended it beyond the limits which I have assumed. There are many, very many well-known hymns, which are found in all our collections, and to which I have not given a place here. Had I purposed to print the originals of all well-known hymns, this book would have greatly outgrown its present size. I have faithfully tried to gather within these covers what a catholic taste would accept as the prime favorites of the church. Of course I have passed over the recent rich additions to our hymnology, except to give in their full form a few of the best. For though we are leaving behind us the era of Cowper and Newton and Watts, let it not be thought that the church is losing its gift of song. It seems to me, that in the elements of tenderness and devoutness, if not in the grand uplift and thrill of the older hymn writers, nothing finer has come from the hearts of men, than "Abide with me, fast falls the even-tide;" "Sun of my soul thou Saviour dear;" "I heard the voice of Jesus say;" "Lead kindly Light, amid th' encircling gloom;" "Nearer my God to Thee;"

"Father, I know that all my life." Hymns like these and others not inferior to them, are the earnest of the Spirit, and the assurance that hymns can no more die out of the Church than can the deep and full experience of the love of Christ. Such names as Heber, and Milman, and the Carys, and Bonar, and Keble, and Kelly, and Grant, and Coxe, and Palmer, and Lyte, and Elliott, and Steele, and Waring, and Kimball, and Seagrave, and Neale are enough, even without the scores that might be added to them; we need no more evidence than they furnish, that we have not dropped behind the last century in this great gift.

In conclusion I would express my grateful acknowledgments to those friends who have responded to my request to send me lists of their favorite hymns, and whose judgment has been a corroboration of my own. More especially let me mention Rev. William Fleming Stevenson, of Dublin, Ireland, whose labors in the department of poetical biography have been so serviceable to me in the preparation of this book. In the library of Harvard College I found a unique collection of hymnological words: and I am under special indebtedness to Mr. Sibley for the use of them. Still greater are my obligations to Sir Roundel Palmer's Book of Praise: which has been to me a great comfort and a great help at every stage of the undertaking.

W. L. GAGE.

HARTFORD, Dec. 4, 1873.

Favorite Hymns

IN THEIR ORIGINAL FORM.

I.

O GOD of Jacob, by whose hand
   Thine Israel still is fed,
Who through this weary pilgrimage
   Hast all our fathers led,

To Thee our humble vows we raise,
   To Thee address our prayer,
And in Thy kind and faithful breast,
   Deposit all our care.

If Thou, through each perplexing path,
   Wilt be our constant guide :
If Thou wilt daily bread supply,
   And raiment wilt provide :

If Thou wilt spread thy shield around,
Till these our wanderings cease,
And at our Father's loved abode,
Our souls arrive in peace:

To Thee as to our Covenant God,
We'll our whole selves resign:
And count that not our tenth alone,
But all we have is Thine.
Philip Doddridge, b. 1702, *d.* 1751.

II.

AS when the weary traveller gains
   The height of some o'erlooking hill,
His heart revives, if 'cross the plains
He eyes his home though distant still.

While he surveys the much loved spot,
He slights the space that lies between:
His past fatigues are now forgot,
Because his journey's end is seen.

Thus, when the Christian pilgrim views,
By faith, his mansion in the skies,
The sight his fainting strength renews,
And wings his speed to reach the prize.

The thought of home his spirit cheers,
No more he grieves for troubles past;
Nor any future trial fears,
So he may safe arrive at last.

'Tis there, he says, I am to dwell
With Jesus in the realms of day:
Then I shall bid my cares farewell,
And He shall wipe my tears away.

Jesus on Thee our hope depends,
To lead us on to Thine abode:
Assured our home will make amends
For all our toil while on the road.
John Newton, b. 1725, *d.* 1807.

III.

'TIS my happiness below
   Not to live without the cross,
But the Saviour's power to know,
Sanctifying every loss.
Trials must and will befall:
But with humble faith to see
Love inscribed upon them all—
This is happiness to me.

God in Israel, sows the seeds
Of affliction, pain and toil;
These spring up and choke the weeds
Which would else o'erspread the soil.
Trials make the promise sweet:
Trials give new life to prayer:
Trials bring me to His feet,
Lay me low, and keep me there.

Did I meet no trials here,
No chastisement by the way,
Might I not with reason fear
I should prove a castaway?
Bastards may escape the rod,
Sunk in earthly, vain delight,
But the true-born child of God
Must not, would not, if he might.

William Cowper, b. 1731, *d.* 1800.

IV.

ONE sweetly solemn thought,
　Comes to me o'er and o'er;
I'm nearer home to-day
Than I've ever been before;

Nearer my Father's house
Where the many mansions be;

Nearer the great white throne,
Nearer the jasper sea;

Nearer the bound of life,
Where we lay our burdens down—
Nearer leaving the cross,
Nearer gaining the crown.

But lying dimly between,
Winding down through the night,
Lies the dark and uncertain stream
That leads us at length to the light.

Closer and closer my steps
Come to the dark abysm,
Closer Death to my lips
Presses the awful chrism;

Father perfect my trust!
Strengthen my feeble faith!
Let me feel as I would when I stand
On the shores of the river of death—

Feel as I would were my feet
Even now slipping over the brink;
For it may be I'm nearer home,
Nearer now, than I think.

Phœbe Cary, b. 1825, *d.* 1871

V.

NOT all the blood of beasts,
   On Jewish altars slain,
Could give the guilty conscience peace,
   Or wash away the stain.

But Christ, the heavenly Lamb,
   Takes all our sins away;
A sacrifice of nobler name
   And richer blood than they.

My faith would lay her hand
   On that dear Head of Thine,
While like a penitent I stand,
   And there confess my sin.

My soul looks back to see
   The burdens Thou didst bear,
When hanging on th' accursèd tree,
   And hopes her guilt was there.

Believing, we rejoice
   To see the curse remove,
We bless the Lamb with cheerful voice,
   And sing His bleeding love.

Isaac Watts, b. 1674, d. 1748.

VI.

O FOR a thousand tongues to sing
    My dear Redeemer's praise,
The glories of my God and King,
    The triumphs of His grace.

My gracious Master and my God,
    Assist me to proclaim,
To spread, through all the earth abroad,
    The honors of Thy Name.

Jesus, the Name that charms our fears,
    That bids our sorrows cease;
'Tis music in the sinner's ears,
    'Tis life, and health, and peace!

He speaks, and, listening to His voice,
    New life the dead receive;
The mournful, broken hearts rejoice,
    The humble poor believe.

Hear Him, ye deaf; His praise, ye dumb,
    Your loosened tongues employ;
Ye blind, behold your Saviour come,
    And leap, ye lame, for joy!

Charles Wesley, b. 1708, *d.* 1788.

VII.

How sweet the Name of Jesus sounds
  In a believer's ear!
It soothes his sorrows, heals his wounds,
  And drives away his fear!

It makes the wounded spirit whole,
  And calms the troubled breast;
'Tis manna to the hungry soul,
  And to the weary rest.

Dear Name! the rock on which I build,
  My shield and hiding-place,
My never-failing treasury, filled
  With boundless stores of grace,

By Thee my prayers acceptance gain,
  Although with sin defiled;
Satan accuses me in vain,
  And I am owned a child.

Jesus, my Shepherd, Husband, Friend,
  My Prophet, Priest, and King,
My Lord, my Life, my Way, my End,
  Accept the praise I bring.

Weak is the effort of my heart,
  And cold my warmest thought
But when I see Thee as Thou art,
  I'll praise Thee as I ought.

Till then, I would Thy love proclaim
  With every fleeting breath;
And may the music of Thy Name
  Refresh my soul in death!

John Newton, b. 1725, *d.* 1807.

VIII.

WHEN I survey the wondrous cross
  On which the Prince of glory died,
My richest gain I count but loss,
  And pour contempt on all my pride.

Forbid it, Lord, that I should boast
  Save in the death of Christ, my God;
All the vain things that charm me most
  I sacrifice them to His blood.

See from His head, His hands, His feet
  Sorrow and love flow mingled down!
Did e'er such love and sorrow meet,
  Or thorns compose so rich a crown?

His dying crimson like a robe,
    Spreads o'er his body on the tree:
Then am I dead to all the globe,
    And all the globe is dead to me.

Were the whole realm of nature mine,
    That were a present far too small;
Love so amazing, so divine,
    Demands my soul, my life, my all.
Isaac Watts, b. 1674, *d.* 1748.

IX.

JESUS I love Thy charming name,
    'Tis music to mine ear:
Fain would I sound it out so loud,
That earth and heaven should hear.

Yes Thou art precious to my soul,
My transport and my trust:
Jewels to Thee are gaudy toys,
And gold is sordid dust.

All my capacious powers can wish
In Thee doth richly meet:
Nor to mine eyes is light so dear,
Nor friendship half so sweet.

Thy grace still dwells upon my heart,
And sheds its fragrance there;
The noblest balm of all its wounds,
The cordial of its care.

I'll speak the honors of Thy name,
With my last laboring breath:
Then speechless clasp Thee in my arms,
The antidote of death.
Philip Doddridge, b. 1702, *d.* 1751.

X.

LET me but hear my Saviour say
Strength shall be equal to the day,
Then I rejoice in deep distress,
Leaning on all sufficient grace.

I glory in infirmity,
That Christ's own power may rest on me:
When I am weak, then am I strong,
Grace is my shield, and Christ my song.

I can do all things, or can bear
All sufferings, if my Lord be there;
Sweet pleasures mingle with the pains,
While His left hand my head sustains.

But if the Lord be once withdrawn,
And we attempt the work alone,
When new temptations spring and rise,
We find how great our weakness is.

So Sampson, when his hair was lost,
Met the Philistines to his cost:
Shook his vain limbs with sad surprise,
Made feeble fight and lost his eyes.

Isaac Watts, b. 1674, d. 1748.

XI.

PLUNGED in a gulf of dark despair
   We wretched sinners lay,
Without one cheerful beam of hope,
   Or spark of glimmering day.

With pitying eyes the Prince of Grace
   Beheld our helpless grief:
He saw, and oh! amazing love!
   He ran to our relief.

Down from the shining seats above
   With joyful haste He fled;
Entered the grave in mortal flesh,
   And dwelt among the dead.

He spoiled the powers of darkness thus,
    And broke our iron chains:
Jesus has freed our captive souls
    From everlasting pains.

In vain the baffled prince of hell
    His cursed projects tries:
We that were doomed his endless slaves,
    Are raised above the skies.

Oh! for this love, let rocks and hills
    Their lasting silence break,
And all harmonious human tongues
    The Saviour's praises speak!

Yes we will praise thee, dearest Lord,
    Our souls are all on flame:
Hosanna round the spacious earth
    To thine adored name.

Angels, assist our mighty joys;
    Strike all your harps of gold!
But, when you raise your highest notes,
    His love can ne'er be told.

Isaac Watts, b. 1674, *d.* 1708.

XII.

CHRIST the Lord is risen to-day,
  Sons of men and angels say:
Raise your joys and triumphs high,
Sing, ye heavens, and earth reply.

Love's redeeming work is done,
Fought the fight, the battle won:
Lo! our Sun's eclipse is o'er;
Lo! He sets in blood no more.

Vain the stone, the watch, the seal;
Christ hath burst the gates of hell!
Death in vain forbids His rise;
Christ hath opened Paradise!

Lives again our glorious King:
Where, O Death is now thy sting?
Once He died, our souls to save;
Where thy victory, O Grave?

Soar we now where Christ has led,
Following our exalted Head;
Made like Him, like Him we rise;
Ours the cross, the grave, the skies.

What though once we perished all,
Partners in our parents' fall?

Second life we all receive,
In our Heavenly Adam live.

Risen with Him, we upward move;
Still we seek the things above;
Still pursue, and kiss the Son
Seated on His Father's Throne.

Scarce on earth a thought bestow,
Dead to all we leave below;
Heaven our aim, and loved abode,
Hid our life with Christ in God:

Hid, till Christ our Life appear
Glorious in His members here;
Joined to Him, we then shall shine,
All immortal, all divine.

Hail the Lord of Earth and Heaven!
Praise to Thee by both be given!
Thee we greet triumphant now!
Hail, the Resurrection Thou!

King of glory, Soul of bliss!
Everlasting life is this,
Thee to know, Thy power to prove,
Thus to sing, and thus to love!

Charles Wesley, b. 1708, d. 1788.

XIII.

JOIN all the glorious names
  Of wisdom, love, and power,
That ever mortals knew,
  That angels ever bore;
All are too mean to speak His worth.
Too mean to set my Saviour forth.

But oh! what gentle terms,
  What condescending ways,
Doth our Redeemer use
  To teach His heavenly grace!
Mine eyes with joy and wonder see
What forms of love He bears for me.

Arrayed in mortal flesh
  He like an Angel stands,
And holds the promises
  And pardons in His hands;
Commissioned from His Father's throne
To make His grace to mortals known.

Great Prophet of my God,
  My tongue would bless Thy Name;
By Thee the joyful news
  Of our salvation came;
The joyful news of sins forgiven,
Of hell subdued, and peace with Heaven.

Be Thou my Counsellor,
My Pattern, and my Guide;
And through this desert land
Still keep me near Thy side:
Oh, let my feet ne'er run astray,
Nor rove, nor seek the crooked way.

I love my Shepherd's voice;
His watchful eyes shall keep
My wandering soul among
The thousands of His sheep;
He feeds His flock, He calls their names,
His bosom bears the tender lambs.

To this dear Surety's hand
Will I commit my cause;
He answers and fulfils
His Father's broken laws:
Behold my soul at freedom set;
My Surety paid the dreadful debt.

Jesus, my great High-Priest,
Offered His Blood and died;
My guilty conscience seeks
No sacrifice beside:
His powerful Blood did once atone,
And now it pleads before the Throne.

My advocate appears
For my defence on high;
The Father bows His ears
And lays His thunder by:
Not that all hell or sin can say
Shall turn His heart, His love away.

My dear Almighty Lord,
My Conqueror and my King,
Thy sceptre and Thy sword,
Thy reigning grace, I sing:
Thine is the power: behold I sit
In willing bonds before Thy feet!

Now let my soul arise,
And tread the Tempter down;
My Captain leads me forth
To conquest and a crown;
A feeble saint shall win the day,
Though death and hell obstruct the way.

Should all the hosts of death
And powers of hell unknown
Put their most dreadful forms
Of rage and mischief on,
I shall be safe; for Christ displays
Superior power, and guardian grace.

Isaac Watts, b. 1674, *d.* 1748.

XIV.

Hail to the Lord's Anointed,
  Great David's greater Son!
Hail, in the time appointed,
  His reign on earth begun!
He comes to break oppression,
  To let the captive free,
To take away transgression,
  And rule in equity.

By such shall he be feared,
  While sun and moon endure,
Beloved, obeyed, revered,
  For he shall judge the poor.
Through changing generations
  With mercy, justice, truth,
While stars maintain their stations,
  Or moons renew their youth.

He comes with succor speedy,
  To those who suffer wrong;
To help the poor and needy,
  And bid the weak be strong:
To give them songs for sighing,
  Their darkness turn to light,
Whose souls, condemned and dying,
  Were precious in His sight.

He shall come down like showers
　　Upon the fruitful earth,
And love, joy, hope, like flowers,
　　Spring in His path to birth ;
Before Him, on the mountains,
　　Shall peace, the herald, go,
And righteousness, in fountains,
　　From hill to valley flow.

Arabia's desert-ranger
　　To Him shall bow the knee;
The Ethiopian stranger
　　His glory come to see :
With offerings of devotion
　　Ships from the Isles shall meet,
To pour the wealth of ocean
　　In tribute at His feet.

Kings shall fall down before Him,
　　And gold and incense bring;
All nations shall adore Him,
　　His praise all people sing;
For He shall have dominion
　　O'er river, sea and shore;
Far as the eagle's pinion,
　　Or dove's light wing, can soar.

For Him shall prayer unceasing,
    And daily vows ascend,
His kingdom still increasing,
    A kingdom without end:
The mountain-dews shall nourish
    A seed, in weakness sown,
Whose fruit shall spread and flourish,
    And shake like Lebanon.

O'er every foe victorious
    He on His throne shall rest,
From age to age more glorious,
    All blessing and all-blest:
The tide of time shall never
    His covenant remove;
His Name shall stand forever,
    That Name to us is Love.
          James Montgomery, b. 1771, *d.* 1854.

XV.

JESUS shall reign where'er the sun
    Does his successive journeys run;
His kingdom stretch from shore to shore,
Till moons shall wax and wane no more.

Behold the islands with their kings,
And Europe, her best tribute brings;

From north to south, the princes meet,
To pay their homage at his feet.

There Persia, glorious to behold,
There India shines, in eastern gold,
And barbarous nations at his word
Submit and bow, and own their Lord.

For Him shall endless prayer be made,
And praises throng to crown His Head;
His Name, like sweet perfume, shall rise
With every morning sacrifice.

People and realms of every tongue
Dwell on His love with sweetest song,
And infant voices shall proclaim
Their early blessings on His Name.

Blessings abound where'er He reigns;
The prisoner leaps to lose his chains;
The weary find eternal rest,
And all the sons of want are blest.

Where He displays His healing power,
Death and the curse are known no more;
In Him the tribes of Adam boast
More blessings than their father lost.

Let every creature rise, and bring
Peculiar honors to our King;
Angels descend with songs again,
And earth repeat the long Amen!
Isaac Watts, b. 1674. *d.* 1748.

XVI.

FROM Greenland's icy mountains,
   From India's coral strand,
Where Afric's sunny fountains
   Roll down their golden sand,
From many an ancient river,
   From many a palmy plain,
They call us to deliver
   Their land from error's chain.

What though the spicy breezes
   Blow soft o'er Java's isle;
Though every prospect pleases,
   And only man is vile;
In vain with lavish kindness
   The gifts of God are strown;
The heathen in his blindness
   Bows down to wood and stone.

Can we, whose souls are lighted
   With wisdom from on high,

Can we to men benighted
  The lamp of life deny?
Salvation! O salvation!
  The joyful sound proclaim,
Till each remotest nation
  Has learn'd Messiah's Name.

Waft, waft, ye winds, His story,
  And you, ye waters, roll,
Till like a sea of glory
  It spreads from pole to pole;
Till o'er our ransomed nature
  The Lamb for sinners slain,
Redeemer, King, Creator,
  In bliss returns to reign.

Bishop Reginald Heber, b. 1783, d. 1826.

XVII.

COME, Holy Spirit, come,
  Let Thy bright beams arise,
Dispel the darkness from our minds,
  And open all our eyes.

Cheer our desponding hearts,
  Thou heavenly Paraclete;
Give us to lie, with humble hope,
  At our Redeemer's feet.

Revive our drooping faith,
Our doubts and fears remove,
And kindle in our breasts the flame
Of never-dying love.

Convince us of our sin,
Then lead to Jesus' blood,
And to our wondering view reveal
The secret love of God.

Show us that loving Man
That rules the courts of bliss,
The Lord of hosts, the Mighty God,
The Eternal Prince of Peace.

'T is Thine to cleanse the heart,
To sanctify the soul,
To pour fresh life in every part,
And new-create the whole.

Dwell therefore in our hearts,
Our minds from bondage free;
Then we shall know, and praise, and love
The Father, Son, and Thee!

Joseph Hart, b. 1712, d. 1768.

XVIII.

GLORIOUS things of thee are spoken,
    Zion, city of our God;
He, whose word cannot be broken,
    Formed thee for His own abode:
On the Rock of Ages founded,
    What can shake thy sure repose?
With salvation's walls surrounded,
    Thou mayst smile at all thy foes.

See, the streams of living waters,
    Springing from eternal love,
Well supply thy sons and daughters,
    And all fear of want remove:
Who can faint, while such a river
    Ever flows thy thirst to assuage;
Grace, which, like the Lord the giver,
    Never fails from age to age?

Round each habitation hovering,
    See the cloud and fire appear,
For a glory and a covering;
    Showing that the Lord is near.
Thus deriving from their banner
    Light by night, and shade by day,
Safe they feed upon the manna,
    Which He gives them when they pray.

Blest inhabitants of Zion,
    Washed in the Redeemer's blood,
Jesus, whom their souls rely on,
    Makes them kings and priests to God.
'Tis His love His people raises
    Over self to reign as kings,
And as priests, His solemn praises
    Each for a thank-offering brings.

Saviour, if of Zion's city
    I, through grace, a member am,
Let the world deride or pity,
    I will glory in Thy Name:
Fading is the worldling's pleasure,
    All his boasted pomp and show;
Solid joys and lasting treasure
    None but Zion's children know.
              John Newton, b. 1725, *d.* 1807.

XIX.

YE servants of the Lord,
    Each in his office wait,
Observant of His heavenly word,
    And watchful at His gate.

Let all your lamps be bright,
    And trim the golden flame;

Gird up your loins, as in His sight,
  For awful is His name.

Watch; 't is your Lord's command;
  And, while we speak, He's near;
Mark the first signal of His hand,
  And ready all appear.

O happy servant he,
  In such a posture found!
He shall his Lord with rapture see,
  And be with honor crowned.

Christ shall the banquet spread
  With His own Royal hand;
And raise that favorite servant's head
  Amid the angelic band.
Philip Doddridge, b. 1702, *d.* 1751.

XX.

COME, we that love the Lord,
  And let our joys be known;
Join in a song with sweet accord,
  And thus surround the throne.

The sorrows of the mind
Be banished from the place:

Religion never was designed
  To make our pleasures less.

Let those refuse to sing
That never knew our God;
But favorites of the Heavenly King
  May speak their joys abroad.

The God that rules on high,
  And thunders when he please,
That rides upon the stormy sky,
  And manages the seas,

This awful God is ours,
  Our Father and our love,
He shall send down His heavenly powers
  To carry us above.

There we shall see His face,
  And never, never sin:
There, from the rivers of His grace
  Drink endless pleasures in.

Yes, and before we rise
  To that immortal state,
The thoughts of such amazing bliss
  Should constant joys create.

The men of grace have found
  Glory begun below;
Celestial fruits on earthly ground
  From faith and hope may grow.

The hill of Zion yields
  A thousand sacred sweets,
Before we reach the heavenly fields,
  Or walk the golden streets.

Then let our songs abound,
  And every tear be dry:
We 're marching through Emmanuel's ground
  To fairer worlds on high.
                Isaac Watts, b. 1674, *d.* 1748.

XXI.

JESUS, where'er Thy people meet,
  There they behold Thy mercy-seat;
Where'er they seek Thee, Thou art found,
And every place is hallowed ground.

For Thou, within no walls confined,
Inhabitest the humble mind;
Such ever bring Thee where they come,
And going take Thee to their home.

Dear Shepherd of Thy chosen few,
Thy former mercies here renew;
Here to our waiting hearts proclaim
The sweetness of Thy saving Name.

Here may we prove the power of prayer
To strengthen faith, and sweeten care,
To teach our faint desires to rise,
And bring all Heaven before our eyes.

Behold, at Thy commanding word,
We stretch the curtain and the cord;
Come Thou, and fill this wider space,
And bless us with a large increase.

Lord, we are few, but Thou art near;
Nor short Thine arm, nor deaf Thine ear;
O rend the heavens, come quickly down,
And make a thousand hearts Thine own!
William Cowper, b. 1731, d. 1800.

XXII.

MY soul, repeat His praise
Whose mercies are so great,
Whose anger is so slow to rise,
   So ready to abate.

God will not always chide:
And when His strokes are felt,
His strokes are fewer than our crimes,
And lighter than our guilt.

High as the heavens are raised
Above the ground we tread,
So far the riches of His grace
Our highest thoughts exceed.

. His power subdues our sins;
And His forgiving love,
Far as the east is from the west,
Doth all our guilt remove.

The pity of the Lord
To those that fear His Name,
Is such as tender parents feel;
He knows our feeble frame.

He knows we are but dust,
Scattered with every breath;
His anger, like a rising wind,
Can send us swift to death.

Our days are as the grass,
Or like the morning flower;
If one sharp blast sweep o'er the field,
It withers in an hour.

But Thy compassions, Lord,
To endless years endure,
And children's children ever find
Thy words of promise sure.

Isaac Watts, b. 1674, *d.* 1748.

XXIII.

THERE is a fountain filled with blood
    Drawn from Emmanuel's veins;
And sinners plunged beneath that flood
    Lose all their guilty stains.

The dying thief rejoiced to see
    That fountain in his day;
And there have I, as vile as he,
    Washed all my sins away.

Dear dying Lamb! Thy precious Blood
    Shall never lose its power,
Till all the ransomed Church of God
    Be saved, to sin no more.

E'er since, by faith, I saw the stream
    Thy flowing wounds supply,
Redeeming love has been my theme,
    And shall be till I die.

Then in a nobler, sweeter song
    I 'll sing Thy power to save,
When this poor lisping, stammering tongue
    Lies silent in the grave.

Lord, I believe Thou hast prepared,
    Unworthy though I be,
For me a blood-bought free reward,
    A golden harp for me:

'T is strung, and tuned for endless years,
    And formed by power divine,
To sound in God the Father's ears
    No other Name but Thine.
William Cowper, b. 1731, d. 1800.

XXIV.

ROCK of Ages, cleft for me,
    Let me hide myself in Thee!
Let the water and the blood,
From Thy riven side which flowed,
Be of sin the double cure,
Cleanse me from i's guilt and power.

Not the labors of my hands
Can fulfil Thy law's demands;

Could my zeal no respite know,
Could my tears forever flow,
All for sin could not atone
Thou must save, and Thou alone.

Nothing in my hand I bring;
Simply to Thy Cross I cling;
Naked, come to Thee for dress;
Helpless, look to Thee for grace;
Foul, I to the Fountain fly;
Wash me, Saviour, or I die!

While I draw this fleeting breath,
When my eyestrings break in death,
When I soar through tracts unknown,
See Thee on Thy judgment-throne;
Rock of Ages, cleft for me,
Let me hide myself in Thee!
Augustus Montague Toplady, b. 1740, d. 1778.

XXV.

WHY do we mourn departing friends,
  Or shake at death's alarms?
'Tis but the voice that Jesus sends
  To call them to His arms.

Are we not tending upward too,
  As fast as time can move?
Nor would we wish the hours more slow
  To keep us from our love.

Why should we tremble to convey
  Their bodies to the tomb?
There the dear flesh of Jesus lay,
  And left a long perfume.

The graves of all His saints He blessed,
  And softened every bed:
Where should the dying members rest,
  But with the dying head?

Thence He arose, ascending high,
  And showed our feet the way;
Up to the Lord our flesh shall fly
  At the great rising day.

Then let the last loud trumpet sound,
  And bid our kindred rise:
Awake, ye nations under ground!
  Ye saints, ascend the skies!
Isaac Watts, b. 1674, *d.* 1748.

XXVI.

RISE, my soul, and stretch thy wings,
   Thy better portion trace;
Rise from transitory things
   Towards Heaven, thy native place.
Sun and moon and stars decay;
Time shall soon this earth remove;
Rise, my soul, and haste away
   To seats prepared above.

Rivers to the ocean run,
   Nor stay in all their course;
Fire ascending seeks the sun;
   Both speed them to their source:
So my soul, derived from God,
Pants to view His glorious face,
Forward tends to His abode,
   To rest in His embrace.

Fly me Riches, fly me Cares,
   Whilst I that coast explore;
Flattering world, with all thy snares
   Solicit me no more!
Pilgrims fix not here their home:
Strangers tarry but a night;
When the last dear morn is come,
   They'll rise to joyful light.

Cease, ye pilgrims, cease to mourn;
   Press onward to the prize;
Soon our Saviour will return
   Triumphant in the skies.
Yet a season, and you know
Happy entrance will be given,
All our sorrows left below,
   And earth exchanged for heaven.
Robert Seagrave, b. 1693, d. unknown.

XXVII.

OUR God, our help in ages past,
   Our hope for years to come,
Our shelter from the stormy blast,
   And our eternal home:

Under the shadow of Thy Throne
   Thy saints have dwelt secure;
Sufficient is Thine arm alone,
   And our defence is sure.

Before the hills in order stood,
   Or earth received her frame,
From everlasting Thou art God,
   To endless years the same.

Thy word commands our flesh to dust,
   "Return ye sons of men:"

All nations rose from earth at first,
    And turn to earth again.

A thousand ages in Thy sight
    Are like an evening gone;
Short as the watch that ends the night
    Before the rising sun.

The busy tribes of flesh and blood,
    With all their lives and cares,
Are carried downwards by Thy flood,
    And lost in following years.

Time, like an ever-rolling stream,
    Bears all its sons away;
They fly forgotten, as a dream
    Dies at the opening day.

Like flowery fields the nations stand,
    Pleased with the morning light:
The flowers, beneath the mower's hand,
    Lie withering ere 'tis night.

Our God, our help in ages past;
    Our hope for years to come;
Be Thou our guard while troubles last,
    And our eternal home!

        Isaac Watts, b. 1674, *d.* 1748.

XXVIII.

PRAYER is the soul's sincere desire,
  Uttered, or unexpressed;
The motion of a hidden fire
  That trembles in the breast.

Prayer is the burthen of a sigh,
  The falling of a tear,
The upward glancing of the eye,
  When none but God is near.

Prayer is the simplest form of speech
  That infant lips can try;
Prayer the sublimest strains that reach
  The Majesty on high.

Prayer is the contrite sinner's voice
  Returning from his ways,
While angels in their songs rejoice,
  And cry, Behold, he prays!

Prayer is the Christian's vital breath,
  The Christian's native air;
His watchword at the gates of death;
  He enters Heaven with prayer.

The saints, in prayer, appear as one
  In word, and deed, and mind;
While with the Father and the Son
  Sweet fellowship they find.

Nor prayer is made by man alone:
  The Holy Spirit pleads;
And Jesus, on the eternal Throne,
  For mourners intercedes.

O Thou, by whom we come to God!
  The Life, the Truth, the Way!
The path of prayer Thyself hast trod:
  Lord! teach us how to pray!
                James Montgomery, b. 1771, *d.* 1854.

XXIX.

WHEN all Thy mercies, O my God,
  My rising soul surveys,
Transported with the view, I'm lost
  In wonder, love, and praise.

O how shall words with equal warmth
  The gratitude declare,
That glows within my ravished heart!
  But Thou canst read it there.

Thy Providence my life sustained,
   And all my wants redrest,
When in the silent womb I lay,
   And hung upon the breast.

To all my weak complaints and cries
   Thy mercy lent an ear,
Ere yet my feeble thoughts had learnt
   To form themselves in prayer.

Unnumbered comforts to my soul
   Thy tender care bestowed,
Before my infant heart conceived
   From whence these comforts flowed.

When in the slippery paths of youth
   With heedless steps I ran,
Thine arm, unseen, conveyed me safe,
   And led me up to man.

Through hidden dangers, toils, and death,
   It gently cleared my way;
And through the pleasing snares of vice,
   More to be feared than they.

When worn with sickness, oft hast Thou
   With health renewed my face;
And, when in sins and sorrows sunk,
   Revived my soul with grace.

Thy bounteous hand with worldly bliss
    Has made my cup run o'er;
And in a kind and faithful friend
    Has doubled all my store.

Ten thousand thousand precious gifts
    My daily thanks employ;
Nor is the least a cheerful heart
    That tastes those gifts with joy.

Through every period of my life
    Thy goodness I'll pursue;
And after death, in distant worlds,
    The glorious theme renew.

When nature fails, and day and night
    Divide thy works no more,
My ever-grateful heart, O Lord,
    Thy mercy shall adore.

Through all eternity to Thee
    A joyful song I'll raise:
But oh! eternity's too short
    To utter all Thy praise!

Joseph Addison, b. 1672, *d.* 1719.

XXX.

COME, my soul, Thy suit prepare;
Jesus loves to answer prayer:
He Himself has bid thee pray,
Therefore will not say thee nay.

Thou art coming to a King,
Large petitions with thee bring;
For His grace and power are such,
None can ever ask too much.

With my burden I begin;
Lord, remove this load of sin;
Let Thy blood, for sinners spilt,
Set my conscience free from guilt.

Lord, I come to Thee for rest;
Take possession of my breast;
There Thy blood-bought right maintain,
And without a rival reign.

As the image in the glass
Answers the beholder's face,
Thus unto my heart appear,
Print Thine own resemblance there.

While I am a pilgrim here,
Let Thy love my spirit cheer;
As my Guide, my Guard, my Friend,
Lead me to my journey's end.

Show me what I have to do;
Every hour my strength renew;
Let me live a life of faith;
Let me die Thy people's death.
John Newton, b. 1725, d. 1807.

XXXI.*

MY faith looks up to Thee,
 Thou Lamb of Cavalry,
  Saviour divine!
Now hear me while I pray;
Take all my guilt away;
O let me from this day
  Be wholly Thine!

May Thy rich grace impart
Strength to my fainting heart,
  My zeal inspire!
As Thou hast died for me,

---

* The only change which I have met with in this hymn, is the substitution of distress for distrust in the last stanza.

O may my love to Thee
Pure, warm, and changeless be,
   A living fire!

While life's dark maze I tread,
And griefs around me spread,
   Be Thou my Guide!
Bid darkness turn to day,
Wipe sorrow's tears away,
Nor let me ever stray
   From Thee aside.

When ends life's transient dream,
When death's cold sullen stream
   Shall o'er me roll;
Blest Saviour! then in love
Fear and distrust remove;
O bear me safe above,
   A ransomed soul!

Ray Palmer, b. 1808.

XXXII.

NOW it belongs not to my care
   Whether I die or live;
To love and serve Thee is my share,
   And this Thy grace must give.

THEIR ORIGINAL FORM.

If death shall bruise this springing seed
    Before it comes to fruit,
The will with Thee goes for the deed,
    Thy life was in the root.

Would I long bear my heavy load,
    And keep my sorrows long?
Would I long sin against my God,
    And His dear mercy wrong?

How much is sinful flesh my foe,
    That doth my soul pervert
To linger here in sin and woe,
    And steals from God my heart!

Christ leads me through no darker rooms
    Than He went through before;
He that unto God's Kingdom comes
    Must enter by this door.

Come, Lord, when grace hath made me meet
    Thy blessed face to see;
For, if Thy work on earth be sweet,
    What will Thy glory be?

Then I shall end my sad complaints,
    And weary sinful days,
And join with the triumphant saints
    That sing Jehovah's praise.

My knowledge of that life is small;
The eye of faith is dim;
But it's enough that Christ knows all,
And I shall be with Him.
Richard Baxter, b. 1615, *d.* 1691.

XXXIII.

O FOR an heart to praise my God,
  A heart from sin set free!
A heart that always feels Thy Blood,
  So freely spilt for me!

An heart resigned, submissive, meek,
  My dear Redeemer's throne;
Where only Christ is heard to speak,
  Where Jesus reigns alone.

An humble, lowly, contrite heart,
  Believing, true, and clean:
Which neither life nor death can part
  From Him that dwells within:

An heart in every thought renewed,
  And full of love divine;
Perfect, and right, and pure, and good,
  A copy, Lord of Thine.

My heart, Thou know'st, can never rest
  Till Thou create my peace:
Till of my Eden re-possessed,
  From every sin I cease.

Fruit of Thy gracious lips, on me
  Bestow that fruit unknown:
The hidden manna, and the tree
  Of life and the white stone.

Thy nature, gracious Lord, impart;
  Come quickly from above;
Write Thy new Name upon my heart,
  Thy new, best Name of Love.
         Charles Wesley, b. 1708, *d.* 1788.

XXXIV.

WHEN I survey life's varied scene,
    Amid the darkest hours
Sweet rays of comfort shine between,
  And thorns are mixed with flowers.

Lord, teach me to adore Thy hand,
  From whence my comforts flow,
And let me in this desert land
  A glimpse of Canaan know.

Is health and ease my happy share!
  O may I bless my God;
Thy kindness let my songs declare,
  And spread Thy praise abroad.

While such delightful gifts as these
  Are kindly lent to me,
Be all my hours of health and ease
  Devoted, Lord, to Thee.

In griefs and pains Thy sacred word,
  (Dear solace of my soul!)
Celestial comforts can afford,
  And all their power control.

When present sufferings pain my heart,
  Or future terrors rise,
And light and hope almost depart
  From these dejected eyes:

Thy powerful word supports my hope,
  Sweet cordial of the mind!
And bears my fainting spirit up,
  And bids me wait resigned.

And Oh! whate'er of earthly bliss
  Thy sovereign hand denies,
Accepted at Thy throne of grace
  Let this petition rise:

Give me a calm, a thankful heart,
  From every murmur free;
The blessings of Thy grace impart,
  And let me live to Thee.

Let the sweet hope that Thou art mine
  My path of life attend,
Thy presence through my journey shine,
  And bless its happy end!

Anne Steele, b. 1717, d. 1778.

XXXV.

THY way, not mine, O Lord,
  However dark it be!
Lead me by Thine own hand,
  Choose out the path for me.

Smooth let it be or rough,
  It will be still the best;
Winding or straight, it leads
  Right onward to Thy rest.

I dare not choose my lot;
  I would not, if I might;
Choose Thou for me, my God;
  So shall I walk aright.

The kingdom that I seek
  Is Thine; so let the way
That leads to it be Thine;
  Else I must surely stray.

Take Thou my cup, and it
  With joy or sorrow fill,
As best to Thee may seem;
  Choose Thou my good and ill;

Choose Thou for me my friends,
  My sickness or my health;
Choose Thou my cares for me,
  My poverty or wealth.

Not mine, not mine the choice,
  In things or great or small;
Be Thou my guide, my strength,
  My wisdom, and my all.
Horatius Bonar, b. 1808.

XXXVI.

FATHER, I know that all my life
  Is portioned out for me,
And the changes that are sure to come
  I do not fear to see;
But I ask Thee for a present mind,
  Intent on pleasing thee.

I ask Thee for a thoughtful love,
  Through constant watching wise,
To meet the glad with joyful smiles
  And wipe the weeping eyes;
And a heart at leisure from itself,
  To soothe and sympathize.

I would not have the restless will
  That hurries to and fro;
Seeking for some great thing to do,
  Or secret thing to know:
I would be treated as a child,
  And guided where I go.

Wherever in the world I am,
  In whatsoe'er estate,
I have a fellowship with hearts
  To keep and cultivate,
And a work of lowly love to do,
  For the Lord on whom I wait.

So I ask Thee for the daily strength
  To none that ask denied,
And a mind to blend with outward life,
  While keeping at Thy side;
Content to fill a little space,
  If Thou be glorified.

And if some things I do not ask
  In my cup of blessing be,
I would have my spirit filled the more
  With grateful love to Thee;
More careful, not to serve Thee much,
  But to please Thee perfectly.

There are briers besetting every path,
  That call for patient care;
There is a cross in every lot,
  And an earnest need for prayer;
But a lowly heart, that leans on Thee
  Is happy anywhere.

In a service which Thy will appoints
  There are no bonds for me;
For my inmost heart is taught the Truth
  That makes Thy children free;
And a life of self-renouncing love
  Is a life of liberty.
               Anna Latitia Waring, b. unknown.

XXXVII.

QUIET, Lord, my froward heart,
    Make me teachable and mild,
Upright, simple, free from art,
    Make me as a weanèd child,
From distrust and envy free,
Pleased with all that pleases Thee.

What Thou shalt to-day provide,
    Let me as a child receive;
What to-morrow may betide
    Calmly to Thy wisdom leave;
'Tis enough that Thou wilt care;
Why should I the burden bear?

As a little child relies
    On a care beyond his own,
Knows he's neither strong nor wise,
    Fears to stir a step alone;
Let me thus with Thee abide,
As my Father, Guard, and Guide.

Thus, preserved from Satan's wiles,
    Safe from dangers, free from fears,
May I live upon Thy smiles
    Till the promised hour appears,
When the sons of God shall prove
    All their Father's boundless love!

John Newton, b. 1725, *d.* 1807.

XXXVIII.

JESUS, cast a look on me;
　Give me sweet simplicity,
Make me poor and keep me low,
Seeking only Thee to know.

Weanèd from my lordly self,
Weanèd from the miser's pelf,
Weanèd from the scorner's ways,
Weanèd from the lust of praise.

All that feeds my busy pride,
Cast it evermore aside;
Bid my will to Thine submit;
Lay me humbly at Thy feet.

Make me like a little child,
Of my strength and wisdom spoiled,
Seeing only in Thy light,
Walking only in Thy might,

Leaning on Thy loving breast,
Where a weary soul may rest;
Feeling well the peace of God
Flowing from Thy gracious Blood!

In this posture let me live,
And hosannas daily give;
In this temper let me die,
And hosannas ever cry!

John Berridge, b. 1716, *d.* 1793.

XXXIX.

THE Lord my Shepherd is,
   I shall be well supplied;
Since He is mine, and I am His,
   What can I want beside?

He leads me to the place
   Where heavenly pasture grows,
Where living waters gently pass,
   And full salvation flows.

If e'er I go astray,
   He doth my soul reclaim,
And guides me in His own right way
   For His most holy Name.

While He affords His aid,
   I cannot yield to fear;
Though I should walk through death's dark shade,
   My Shepherd's with me there.

In spite of all my foes
Thou dost my table spread;
My cup with blessings overflows,
And joy exalts my head.

The bounties of Thy love
Shall crown my following days;
Nor from Thy house will I remove,
Nor cease to speak Thy praise.
Isaac Watts, b. 1674, *d.* 1748.

XL.

JESU, lover of my soul,
  Let me to Thy bosom fly,
While the nearer waters roll,
  While the tempest still is high!
Hide me, O my Saviour, hide,
  Till the storm of life is past,
Safe into the haven guide;
  O receive my soul at last!

Other refuge have I none;
  Hangs my helpless soul on Thee;
Leave, ah! leave me not alone,
  Still support and comfort me!

All my trust on Thee is stayed,
    All my help from Thee I bring:
Cover my defenceless head
    With the shadow of Thy wing!

Wilt Thou not regard my call?
    Wilt Thou not accept my prayer?
Lo! I sink, I faint, I fall!
    Lo! on Thee I cast my care!
Reach me out Thy gracious hand!
    While I of Thy strength receive,
Hoping against hope I stand,
    Dying, and behold I live!

Thou, O Christ, art all I want;
    More than all in Thee I find:
Raise the fallen, cheer the faint,
    Heal the sick, and lead the blind!
Just and holy is Thy Name;
    I am all unrighteousness;
False and full of sin I am,
    Thou art full of truth and grace.

Plenteous grace with Thee is found,
    Grace to cover all my sin;
Let the healing streams abound;
    Make and keep me pure within!

Thou of Life the Fountain art,
　Freely let me take of Thee;
Spring Thou up within my heart!
　Rise to all eternity!
Charles Wesley, b. 1708, d. 1788.

XLI.

CHRIST, whose glory fills the skies,
　　Christ, the true, the only Light,
Sun of Righteousness, arise,
　Triumph o'er the shades of night!
Day-spring from on high, be near!
Day-star, in my heart appear!

Dark and cheerless is the morn
　Unaccompanied by Thee;
Joyless is the day's return,
　Till Thy mercy's beams I see;
Till they inward light impart,
Glad my eyes, and warm my heart.

Visit then this soul of mine,
　Pierce the gloom of sin and grief!
Fill me, Radiancy Divine,
　Scatter all my unbelief!
More and more Thyself display,
Shining to the perfect day!
Charles Wesley, b. 1708, d. 1888.

XLII.*

ALL praise to Thee, my God, this night,
For all the blessings of the light;
Keep me, O keep me, King of kings,
Beneath Thine own Almighty wings!

Forgive me, Lord, for Thy dear Son,
The ill that I this day have done;
That with the world, myself, and Thee,
I, ere I sleep, at peace may be.

Teach me to live, that I may dread
The grave as little as my bed!
To die, that this vile body may
Rise glorious at the awful day!

O may my soul on Thee repose;
And may sweet sleep mine eyelids close;
Sleep, that may me more vigorous make
To serve my God when I awake!

When in the night I sleepless lie,
My soul with heavenly thoughts supply!
Let no ill dreams disturb my rest,
No powers of darkness me molest!

---

* It is impossible for me to determine whether Ken originally began this hymn with the words All praise, or with the word Glory. The best authorities are divided.

Dull sleep, of sense me to deprive!
I am but half my time alive:
Thy faithful lovers, Lord, are grieved
To lie so long of Thee bereaved.

But though sleep o'er my frailty reigns,
Let it not hold me long in chains!
And now and then let loose my heart,
Till it an hallelujah dart!

The faster sleep the senses binds,
The more unfettered are our minds;
O may my soul, from matter free,
Thy loveliness unclouded see!

O when shall I, in endless day,
Forever chase dark sleep away,
And hymns with the supernal choir
Incessant sing, and never tire?

O may my Guardian, while I sleep,
Close to my bed his vigils keep;
His love angelical instil;
Stop all the avenues of ill;

May he celestial joy rehearse,
And thought to thought with me converse;
Or in my stead, all the night long,
Sing to my God a grateful song!

Praise God, from whom all blessings flow,
Praise Him, all creatures here below!
Praise Him above, ye heavenly host!
Praise Father, Son, and Holy Ghost!
   Bishop Thomas Ken, b. 1637, *d.* 1711.

XLIII.

SUN of my soul, Thou Saviour dear,
 It is not night if Thou be near;
Oh! may no earth-born cloud arise
To hide Thee from Thy servant's eyes!

When round Thy wondrous works below
My searching rapturous glance I throw,
Tracing out wisdom, power, and love,
In earth or sky, in stream or grove;

Or, by the light Thy words disclose,
Watch time's full river as it flows,
Scanning Thy gracious Providence,
Where not too deep for mortal sense;

When with dear friends sweet talk I hold,
And all the flowers of life unfold;
Let not my heart within me burn,
Except in all I Thee discern!

When the soft dews of kindly sleep
My wearied eyelids gently steep,
Be my last thought, how sweet to rest
Forever on my Saviour's breast!

Abide with me from morn till eve,
For without Thee I cannot live!
Abide with me when night is nigh,
For without Thee I dare not die!

Thou Framer of the light and dark,
Steer through the tempest Thine own ark!
Amid the howling, wintry sea
We are in port if we have Thee.

The rulers of this Christian land,
'Twixt Thee and us ordained to stand,
Guide Thou their course, O Lord, aright!
Let all do all as in Thy sight!

Oh! by Thine own sad burthen, borne
So meekly up the hill of scorn,
Teach Thou Thy priests their daily cross
To bear as Thine, nor count it loss!

If some poor wandering child of Thine
Have spurned, to-day, the voice divine;
Now, Lord, the gracious work begin;
Let him no more lie down in sin!

Watch by the sick, enrich the poor
With blessings from Thy boundless store!
Be every mourner's sleep to night
Like infant's slumbers, pure and light!

Come near and bless us when we wake,
Ere through the world our way we take:
'Till, in the ocean of Thy love.
We lose ourselves in Heaven above!
John Keble, b. 1792, *d.* 1866.

XLIV.

SWEET is the work, my God, my King,
To praise Thy Name, give thanks and sing,
To show Thy love by morning light,
And talk of all Thy truth at night.

Sweet is the day of sacred rest;
No mortal cares shall seize my breast:
O may my heart in tune be found,
Like David's harp of solemn sound!

My heart shall triumph in my Lord,
And bless His works, and bless His word:
Thy works of grace, how bright they shine!
How deep Thy counsels, how divine!

Fools never raise their thoughts so high;
Like brutes they live, like brutes they die;
Like grass they flourish, till Thy breath
Blast them in everlasting death.

But I shall share a glorious part,
When grace hath well refined my heart,
And fresh supplies of joy are shed,
Like holy oil to cheer my head.

Sin, (my worst enemy before,)
Shall vex my eyes and ears no more;
My inward foes shall all be slain,
Nor Satan break my peace again.

Then shall I see and hear and know
All I desired and wished below,
And every power find sweet employ
In that eternal world of joy!

Isaac Watts, b. 1674, *d.* 1748.

XLV.

COME, O thou Traveller unknown,
   Whom still I hold, but cannot see,
My company before is gone,
   And I am left alone with Thee!
With Thee all night I mean to stay,
And wrestle till the break of day.

I need not tell Thee who I am,
    My misery or sin declare;
Thyself hast called me by my name;
    Look on Thy hands, and read it there!
But Who, I ask Thee, Who art Thou?
Tell me Thy Name, and tell me now.

In vain Thou strugglest to get free,
    I never will unloose my hold;
Art Thou the Man that died for me?
    The secret of Thy love unfold.
Wrestling, I will not let Thee go,
Till I Thy Name, Thy Nature know

Wilt Thou not yet to me reveal
    Thy new, unutterable Name!
Tell me, I still beseech Thee, tell;
    To know it now, resolved I am:
Wrestling, I will not let Thee go,
Till I Thy Name, Thy Nature know.

'T is all in vain to hold Thy tongue,
    Or touch the hollow of my thigh;
Though every sinew be unstrung,
    Out of my arms Thou shalt not fly;
Wrestling, I will not let Thee go,
Till I Thy Name, Thy Nature know.

What though my shrinking flesh complain,
   And murmur to contend so long?
I rise superior to my pain;
   When I am weak, then I am strong:
And when my all of strength shall fail,
I shall with the God-Man prevail.

My strength is gone; my nature dies;
   I sink beneath Thy weighty hand,
Faint to revive, and fall to rise;
   I fall, and yet by faith I stand:
I stand, and will not let Thee go,
Till I Thy Name, Thy Nature know.

Yield to me now, for I am weak,
   But confident in self-despair;
Speak to my heart, in blessings speak,
   Be conquered by my instant prayer!
Speak, or Thou never hence shalt move,
And tell me, if Thy Name is Love?

'T is Love! 't is Love! Thou diedst for me!
   I hear Thy whisper in my heart!
The morning breaks, the shadows flee;
   Pure universal Love Thou art!
To me, to all, Thy bowels move!
Thy Nature, and Thy Name, is Love!

My prayer hath power with God; the grace
    Unspeakable I now receive;
Through faith I see Thee face to face,
    I see Thee face to face, and live:
In vain I have not wept and strove;
Thy Nature, and Thy Name, is Love.

I know Thee, Saviour, who Thou art;
    Jesus, the feeble sinner's Friend!
Nor wilt Thou with the night depart,
    But stay, and love me to the end!
Thy mercies never shall remove,
Thy Nature, and Thy Name, is Love!

The Sun of Righteousness on me
    Hath rose, with healing in His wings;
Withered my nature's strength, from Thee
    My soul its life and succor brings;
My help is all laid up above;
Thy Nature, and Thy Name, is Love.

Contented now upon my thigh
    I halt, till life's short journey end;
All helplessness, all weakness, I
    On Thee alone for strength depend;
Nor have I power from Thee to move;
Thy Nature, and Thy Name, is Love.

Lame as I am, I take the prey,
   Hell, earth, and sin, with ease o'ercome;
I leap for joy, pursue my way,
   And as a bounding hart fly home!
Through all eternity to prove,
Thy Nature, and Thy Name, is Love!
Charles Wesley, b. 1708, *d.* 1788.

XLVI.

JESUS, I my cross have taken,
   All to leave, and follow Thee;
Destitute, despised, forsaken,
   Thou, from hence, my all shalt be:
Perish every fond ambition,
   All I've sought, or hoped, or known;
Yet how rich is my condition!
   God and Heaven are still my own!

Let the world despise and leave me,
   They have left my Saviour too;
Human hearts and looks deceive me;
   Thou art not, like them, untrue:
And, while Thou shalt smile upon me,
   God of wisdom, love, and might,
Foes may hate, and friends may shun me;
   Show Thy face, and all is bright!

Go, then. earthly fame and treasure!
　Come, disaster, scorn, and pain!
In Thy service, pain is pleasure,
　With Thy favor, loss is gain!
I have called Thee, Abba, Father!
　I have stayed my heart on Thee!
Storms may howl, and clouds may gather,
　All must work for good to me.

Man may trouble and distress me,
　'Twill but drive me to Thy breast;
Life with trials hard may press me,
　Heaven will bring me sweeter rest!
O, 'tis not in grief to harm me,
　While Thy love is left to me!
O, 't were not in joy to charm me,
　Were that joy unmixed with Thee!

Take, my soul, thy full salvation;
　Rise o'er sin, and fear, and care;
Joy to find, in every station,
　Something still to do or bear:
Think what spirit dwells within thee!
　What a Father's smile is thine!
What a Saviour died to win thee!
　Child of Heaven, shouldst thou repine?

Haste then on from grace to glory,
  Armed by faith, and winged by prayer;
Heaven's eternal day's before thee,
  God's own hand shall guide thee there!
Soon shall close thy earthly mission,
  Swift shall pass thy pilgrim days;
Hope soon change to glad fruition,
  Faith to sight, and prayer to praise!
Henry Francis Lyte, b. 1793, d. 1847.

XLVII.

ABIDE with me! fast falls the even-tide;
  The darkness deepens; Lord, with me abide!
When other helpers fail, and comforts flee,
Help of the helpless, O abide with me!

Swift to its close ebbs out life's little day;
Earth's joys grow dim; its glories pass away;
Change and decay in all around I see;
O Thou, who changest not, abide with me!

Not a brief glance I beg, a passing word;
But, as Thou dwell'st with Thy disciples, Lord,
Familiar, condescending, patient, free,
Come, not to sojourn, but abide, with me!

Come not in terrors, as the King of kings;
But kind and good, with healing in Thy wings;
Tears for all woes, a heart for every plea;
Come, Friend of sinners, and thus 'bide with me!

Thou on my head in early youth didst smile;
And, though rebellious and perverse meanwhile,
Thou hast not left me, oft as I left Thee.
On to the close, O Lord, abide with me!

I need Thy Presence every passing hour:
What but Thy grace can foil the Tempter's power?
Who like Thyself my guide and stay can be?
Through cloud and sunshine, O abide with me!

I fear no foe, with Thee at hand to bless:
Ills have no weight, and tears no bitterness:
Where is death's sting? where, Grave, thy victory?
I triumph still, if Thou abide with me!

Hold then Thy cross before my closing eyes!
Shine through the gloom, and point me to the skies!
Heaven's morning breaks, and earth's vain shadows
 flee;
In life and death, O Lord, abide with me!

Henry Francis Lyte, b. 1793, *d.* 1847.

XLVIII.

COMMIT thou all thy griefs
   And ways into His hands,
To His sure Truth and tender care,
   Who earth and Heaven commands.

Who points the clouds their course,
   Whom winds and seas obey,
He shall direct thy wandering feet,
   He shall prepare thy way.

Thou on the Lord rely;
   So safe shalt thou go on;
Fix on His work thy steadfast **eye**,
   So shall thy work be done.

No profit canst thou gain
   By self-consuming care;
To Him commend thy cause; **His ear**
   Attends the softest prayer.

Thy everlasting Truth,
   Father! Thy ceaseless love,
Sees all Thy children's wants, and knows
   What best for each will prove.

And whatsoe'er Thou will'st
Thou dost, O King of kings;
What Thy unerring wisdom chose,
Thy Power to being brings.

Thou everywhere hast sway,
And all things serve Thy might;
Thy every act pure blessing is,
Thy path unsullied light.

When Thou arisest, Lord,
Who shall Thy work withstand?
When all Thy children want Thou giv'st,
Who, who shall stay Thy hand?

Give to the winds thy fears;
Hope, and be undismayed;
God hears thy sighs, and counts thy tears,
God shall lift up thy head.

Through waves and clouds and storms,
He gently clears thy way;
Wait thou His time; so shall this night
Soon end in joyous day.

Still heavy is thy heart?
Still sink thy spirits down?
Cast off the weight, let fear depart,
And every care be gone.

What though thou rulest not?
Yet Heaven and earth and hell
Proclaim, God sitteth on the Throne,
And ruleth all things well!

Leave to His sovereign sway
To choose and to command;
So shalt thou wondering own, His way
How wise, how strong His hand!

Far, far above thy thought
His counsel shall appear,
When fully He the work hath wrought
That caused thy needless fear.

Thou seest our weakness, Lord!
Our hearts are known to Thee:
Oh! lift Thou up the sinking hand,
Confirm the feeble knee!

Let us, in life, in death,
Thy steadfast Truth declare,
And publish, with our latest breath,
Thy love and guardian care!

John Wesley, b. 1703, *d.* 1791.

XLIX.

YOUR harps, ye trembling saints,
  Down from the willows take;
Loud to the praise of Love divine,
  Bid every string awake.

Though in a foreign land,
  We are not far from home;
And nearer to our house above
  We every moment come.

His Grace will to the end
  Stronger and brighter shine;
Nor present things, nor things to come,
  Shall quench the spark divine.

Fastened within the vail,
  Hope be your anchor strong;
His loving Spirit the sweet gale
  That wafts you smooth along.

Or, should the surges rise,
  And peace delay to come,
Blest is the sorrow, kind the storm,
  That drives us nearer home.

The people of His choice
He will not cast away;
Yet do not always here expect
On Tabor's mount to stay.

When we in darkness walk,
Nor feel the heavenly flame,
Then is the time to trust our God,
And rest upon His Name.

Soon shall our doubts and fears
Subside at His control;
His loving-kindness shall break through
The midnight of the soul.

No wonder, when His Love
Pervades your kindling breast,
You wish forever to retain
The heart-transporting Guest.

Yet learn, in every state,
To make His will your own;
And, when the joys of sense depart,
To walk by faith alone.

By anxious fear depressed,
When from the deep ye mourn,
" Lord, why so hasty to depart,
So tedious in return?"

Still on His plighted Love
At all events rely;
The very hidings of His face
Shall train thee up to joy.

Wait, till the shadows flee;
Wait thy appointed hour;
Wait, till the Bridegroom of thy soul
Reveal His Love with power.

The time of Love will come,
When thou shalt clearly see,
Not only that He shed His Blood,
But that it flowed for thee!

Tarry His leisure, then,
Although He seem to stay;
A moment's intercourse with Him
Thy grief will overpay.

Blest is the man, O God,
That stays himself on Thee!
Who wait for Thy salvation, Lord,
Shall Thy salvation see!

Augustus Montague Toplady, b. **1740,** *d.* **1778.**

L.

FOREVER with the Lord!
　　Amen! so let it be!
Life from the dead is in that word,
　　'T is immortality!

　　Here in the body pent,
　　　　Absent from Him I roam,
　　Yet nightly pitch my moving tent
　　　　A day's march nearer home.

　　My Father's house on high,
　　　　Home of my soul! how near,
　　At times, to faith's far-seeing eye,
　　　　Thy golden gates appear.

　　Ah! then my spirit faints
　　　　To reach the land I love,
　　The bright inheritance of saints,
　　　　Jerusalem above!

　　Yet clouds will intervene,
　　　　And all my prospect flies;
　　Like Noah's dove, I flit between
　　　　Rough seas and stormy skies.

Anon the clouds depart,
  The winds and waters cease;
While sweetly o'er my gladdened heart
  Expands the bow of peace!

Beneath its glowing arch,
  Along the hallowed ground,
I see cherubic armies march,
  A camp of fire around.

I hear at morn and even,
  At noon and midnight hour,
The choral harmonies of Heaven
  Earth's Babel tongues o'erpower.

Then, then I feel, that He,
  Remembered or forgot.
The Lord, is never far from me,
  Though I perceive Him not.
          James Montgomery, b. 1771, d. 1854.

LI.

SONGS of praise the angels sang,
  Heaven with hallelujahs rang,
When Jehovah's work begun,
When He spake and it was done.

Songs of praise awoke the morn,
When the Prince of Peace was born;
Songs of praise awoke when He
Captive led captivity.

Heaven and earth must pass away,
Songs of praise shall crown that day;
God will make new heavens, new earth,
Songs of praise shall hail their birth.

And can man alone be dumb,
Till that glorious kingdom come?
No: the Church delights to raise
Psalms, and hymns, and songs of praise.

Saints below, with heart and voice,
Still in songs of praise rejoice,
Learning here, by faith and love,
Songs of praise to sing above.

Borne upon their latest breath,
Songs of praise shall conquer death;
Then, amidst eternal joy,
Songs of praise their powers employ.

James Montgomery, b. 1771, *d.* 1854.

LII.

FRIEND after friend departs;
  Who hath not lost a friend?
There is no union here of hearts,
  That finds not here an end:
Were this frail world our only rest,
  Living or dying, none were blest.

Beyond the flight of time,
  Beyond this vale of death,
There surely is some blessed clime,
  Where life is not a breath,
Nor life's affections transient fire,
Whose sparks fly upwards to expire.

There is a world above,
  Where parting is unknown;
A whole eternity of love,
  Formed for the good alone:
And faith beholds the dying here
Translated to that happier sphere.

Thus star by star declines
  Till all are passed away,
As morning high and higher shines
  To pure and perfect day;
Nor sink those stars in empty night;
They hide themselves in heaven's own light.

James Montgomery, b. 1771, d. 1854.

LIII.

COME, let us join our cheerful songs
    With angels round the Throne;
Ten thousand thousand are their tongues,
    But all their joys are one.

"Worthy the Lamb that died," they cry,
    "To be exalted thus!"
"Worthy the Lamb!" our lips reply,
    "For He was slain for us."

Jesus is worthy to receive
    Honor and power divine,
And blessings, more than we can give,
    Be, Lord, forever Thine.

Let all that dwell above the sky,
    And air, and earth, and seas,
Conspire to lift Thy glories high,
    And speak Thine endless praise.

The whole Creation join in one
    To bless the sacred Name
Of Him, that sits upon the Throne,
    And to adore the Lamb!

        Isaac Watts, b. 1674, *d.* 1748.

LIV.

JUST as I am, without one plea
But that Thy Blood was shed for me,
And that Thou bidd'st me come to Thee,
   O Lamb of God, I come!

Just as I am, and waiting not
To rid my soul of one dark blot,
To Thee, whose Blood can cleanse each spot,
   O Lamb of God. I come!

Just as I am, though tossed about
With many a conflict, many a doubt,
Fightings and fears within, without,
   O Lamb of God, I come!

Just as I am, poor, wretched, blind,
Sight, riches, healing of the mind,
Yea, all I need, in Thee to find,
   O Lamb of God, I come!

Just as I am, Thou wilt receive,
Wilt welcome, pardon, cleanse, relieve!
Because Thy promise I believe,
   O Lamb of God, I come!

Just as I am, (Thy Love unknown
Has broken every barrier down,)
Now, to be Thine, yea, Thine alone,
  O Lamb of God, I come!

Just as I am, of that free 'ove
The breadth, length, depth, and height to prove,
Here for a season, then above,
  O Lamb of God, I come!
Charlotte Elliott, b. 1789, d. 1871.

LV.

HOW gentle God's commands,
  How kind His precepts are!
Come, cast your burdens on the Lord,
  And trust His constant care.

While Providence supports,
  Let saints securely dwell;
That Hand, which bears all Nature up,
  Shall guide His children well.

Why should this anxious load
  Press down your weary mind?
Haste to your Heavenly Father's throne,
  And sweet refreshment find.

His goodness stands approved
Down to the present day;
I'll drop my burden at His feet,
And bear a song away.
                    Philip Doddridge, b. 1702, d. 1751.

LVI.

THERE is a land of pure delight,
  Where saints immortal reign,
Infinite day excludes the night,
  And pleasures banish pain.

There everlasting spring abides,
  And never withering flowers;
Death, like a narrow sea, divides
  This heavenly land from ours.

Sweet fields beyond the swelling flood
  Stand dressed in living green:
So to the Jews old Canaan stood,
  While Jordan rolled between.

But timorous mortals start and shrink
  To cross this narrow sea,
And linger shivering on the brink,
  And fear to launch away.

O, could we make our doubts remove,
  These gloomy doubts that rise,
And see the Canaan that we love
  With unbeclouded eyes,—

Could we but climb where Moses stood;
  And view the landscape o'er,—
Not Jordan's stream, nor death's cold flood,
  Should fright us from the shore.
                    Isaac Watts, b. 1674, *d.* 1748.

LVII.

ALL hail the power of Jesus' name!
  Let angels prostrate fall;
Bring forth the royal diadem,
  And crown Him Lord of all!

Let high-born seraphs tune the lyre,
  And, as they tune it, fall
Before His face, who tunes their choir,
  And crown Him Lord of all!

Crown Him, ye morning stars of light,
  Who fixed this floating ball;
Now hail the strength of Israel's might,
  And crown Him Lord of all!

Crown Him, ye morning stars of light!
  He fixed this floating ball;

Now hail the strength of Israel's might,
  And crown Him Lord of all!

Crown Him, ye martyrs of our God,
  Who from His altar call!
Extol the Stem of Jesse's rod,
  And crown Him Lord of all!

Ye seed of Israel's chosen race,
  Ye ransomed of the fall,
Hail Him who saved you by His grace,
  And crown Him Lord of all!

Hail Him, ye heirs of David's line,
  Whom David Lord did call;
The God incarnate, Man Divine,
  And crown Him Lord of all!

Sinners, whose love can ne'er forget
  The wormwood and the gall,
Go spread your trophies at His feet,
  And crown Him Lord of all!

Let every tribe and every tongue
  That hear the Saviour's call,
Now shout in universal song,
  And crown Him Lord of all!
            Rev. Edward Perronet, d. 1792.

LVIII.

LOVE Divine, all loves excelling,
    Joy of Heaven, to earth come down,
Fix in us Thy humble dwelling,
    All Thy faithful mercies crown.
Jesus, Thou art all compassion,—
    Pure, unbounded love Thou art;
Visit us with Thy salvation,
    Enter every trembling heart.

Breathe, O breathe Thy loving Spirit
    Into every troubled breast!
Let us all in Thee inherit,
    Let us find that second rest.
Take away the love of sinning;
    Alpha and Omega be;
End of faith, as its beginning,
    Set our hearts at liberty.

Come, Almighty to deliver!
    Let us all Thy life receive;
Suddenly return, and never,
    Never more Thy temples leave.
Thee we would be always blessing,
    Serve Thee as Thy host above;
Pray, and praise Thee without ceasing,
    Glory in Thy perfect love.

Finish, then, Thy new creation;
  Pure and spotless let it be;
Let us see Thy great salvation
  Perfectly secured by Thee,—
Changed from glory into glory,
  Till in heaven we take our place,—
Till we cast our crowns before Thee,
  Lost in wonder, love, and praise!
          Charles Wesley, b. 1708, *d.* 1788.

LIX.

ONE there is, above all others,
  Well deserves the name of friend;
His is love beyond a brother's,
  Costly, free, and knows no end:
They who once His kindness prove,
Find it everlasting love.

Which of all our friends to save us,
  Could or would have shed their blood?
But our Jesus died to have us
  Reconciled in Him to God:
This was boundless love indeed,
Jesus is a friend in need.

Men, when raised to lofty stations,
  Often know their friends no more;

Slight and scorn their poor relations,
    Though they valued them before:
But our Saviour always owns
Those whom He redeemed with groans.

When He lived on earth abasèd,
    Friend of sinners was His name;
Now, above all glory raisèd,
    He rejoices in the same:
Still He calls them brethren, friends,
And to all their wants attends.

Could we bear from one another
    What He daily bears from us?
Yet this glorious Friend and Brother
    Loves us, though we treat him thus:
Though for good we render ill,
He accounts us brethren still.

Oh! for grace our hearts to soften;
    Teach us, Lord, at length to love.
We, alas, forget too often
    What a Friend we have above;
But, when home our souls are brought,
We will love Thee as we ought.

John Newton, b. 1725, *d.* 1807.

THEIR ORIGINAL FORM.   *This 1st 1719 text:*
                              the 1709 is much
           LX.   *different*

ish SING to the Lord with joyful voice;
       Let ev'ry land His name adore;
    The ~~northern~~ isles shall send the noise
       Across the ocean to the shore.

    Nations, attend before His throne
       With solemn fear, with sacred joy:
    Know that the Lord is God alone;
       He can create, and He destroy.

    { ~~Before Jehovah's awful throne,~~
    {   ~~Ye nations, bow with sacred joy:~~
    { ~~Know that the Lord is God alone;~~
    {   ~~He can create, and He destroy.~~ }

    His sovereign power, without our aid,
       Made us of clay, and formed us men;
    And when, like wand'ring sheep, we strayed,
       He brought us to His fold again.

    We are His people, we His care,
       Our souls, and all our mortal frame;
    What lasting honors shall we rear,
       Almighty Maker, to Thy name?
         5

We'll crowd Thy gates with thankful songs,
  High as the heavens our voices raise;
And earth, with her ten thousand tongues,
  Shall fill Thy courts with sounding praise.

Wide as the world is Thy command,
  Vast as eternity, Thy love:
Firm as a rock Thy truth must stand,
  When rolling years shall cease to move.
Isaac Watts, b. 1674, d. 1748.

LXI.

TRIUMPHANT Zion! lift thy head
  From dust and darkness and the dead;
Though humbled long, awake at length,
And gird thee with thy Saviour's strength.

Put all thy beauteous garments on,
And let thy various charms be known:
The world thy glories shall confess,
Decked in the robes of righteousness.

No more shall foes unclean invade,
And fill thy hallowed walls with dread;
No more shall hell's insulting host
Their vict'ry and thy sorrows boast.

God, from on high, thy groans will hear;
His hand thy ruins shall repair;
Reared and adorned by love Divine,
Thy towers and battlements shall shine.

Grace shall dispose my heart and voice
To share and echo back her joys:
Nor will her watchful Monarch cease
To guard her in eternal peace.
Philip Doddridge, b. 1702, *d.* 1751.

LXII.

GOD is the refuge of His saints,
    When storms of sharp distress **invade**;
Ere we can offer our complaints,
    Behold Him present with His aid.

Let mountains from their seats be hurled
    Down to the deep, and buried there;
Convulsions shake the solid world;
    Our faith shall never yield to fear.

Loud may the troubled ocean roar;
    In sacred peace our souls abide;
While every nation, every shore,
    Trembles and dreads the swelling tide.

There is a stream, whose gentle flow
  Supplies the city of our God,
Life, love, and joy, still gliding through,
  And watering our divine abode.

That sacred stream, Thine holy word,
  That all my raging fear controls :
Sweet peace Thy promises afford,
  And give new strength to fainting souls.

Zion enjoys her Monarch's love,
  Secure against a threatening hour;
Nor can her firm foundations move,
  Built on His truth and armed with power.
                    Isaac Watts, b. 1674, *d.* 1748.

LXIII.

AMAZING grace! (how sweet the sound!)
  That saved a wretch like me ;
I once was lost, but now am found,
  Was blind, but now I see.

'T was grace that taught my heart to fear,
  And grace my fears relieved :
How precious did that grace appear,
  The hour I first believed!

Through many dangers, toils, and snares,
    I have already come;
'T is grace has brought me safe thus far,
    And grace will lead me home.

The Lord has promised good to me,
    His word my hope secures:
He will my shield and portion be
    As long as life endures.

Yes! when this flesh and heart shall fail,
    And mortal life shall cease,
I shall possess, within the veil,
    A life of joy and peace.

The earth shall soon dissolve like snow,
    The sun forbear to shine:
But God, who called me here below,
    Will be forever mine.
                  John Newton, b. 1725, d. 1807

LXIII.

OH, help us, Lord!—each hour of need
    Thy heavenly succor give;
Help us in thought, and word, and deed,
    Each hour on earth we live.

Oh, help us when our spirits bleed,
    With contrite anguish sore;
And when our hearts are cold and dead,
    Oh, help us, Lord, the more!

Oh, help us through the prayer of faith,
    More firmly to believe!
For still the more the servant hath,
    The more shall he receive.

If strangers to Thy fold we call,
    Imploring at Thy feet
The crumbs that from Thy table fall,
    'T is all we dare entreat.

But be it, Lord of mercy, all,
    So Thou wilt grant but this:
The crumbs that from Thy table fall,
    Are life, and light, and bliss.

Oh, help us, Jesus! from on high;
    We know no help but Thee;
Oh, help us so to live and die,
    As thine in heaven to be!

Henry Hart Milman, b. 1791, *d.* 1868.

LXIV.

SOW in the morn thy seed,
    At eve hold not thy hand;
To doubt and fear give thou no heed;
    Broad-cast it o'er the land!

Beside all waters sow,
    The highway furrows stock,
Drop it where thorns and thistles grow,
    Scatter it on the rock.

The good, the fruitful ground,
    Expect not here nor there,
O'er hill and dale, by plots, 't is found,
    Go forth, then, everywhere.

Thou know'st not which may thrive,
    The late or early sown:
Grace keeps the precious germs alive,
    When and wherever strown.

Then duly shall appear,
    In verdure, beauty, strength,
The tender blade, the stalk, the ear,
    And the full corn at length.

Thou canst not toil in vain;
  Cold, heat, and moist and dry
Shall foster and mature the grain
  For garners in the sky.

Thence, when the glorious end,
  The day of God, is come,
The angel reapers shall descend,
  And Heaven cry—Harvest-home!

James Montgomery, b. 1771, *d.* 1854.

LXV.

HARK! the herald angels sing,
  " Glory to the new-born King!
Peace on earth, and mercy mild;
God to man is reconciled."

Joyful, all ye nations, rise;
Join the triumphs of the skies;
With th' angelic host proclaim,
" Christ is born in Bethlehem."

Christ, by highest heaven adored;
Christ, the everlasting Lord:
Late in time behold Him come,
Offspring of a Virgin's womb.

Veiled in flesh the Godhead see!
Hail the incarnate Deity!
Pleased as man with man to appear,
Jesus, our Immanuel here!

Hail, the heaven-born Prince of Peace!
Hail, the Sun of Righteousness!
Light and life to all He brings,
Risen with healing in His wings.

Mild He lays His glory by;
Born that man no more may die;
Born to raise the sons of earth;
Born to give them second birth.
Bishop Reginald Heber, b. 1783, d. 1826.

LXVI.

SEE Israel's gentle Shepherd stands
    With all-engaging charms;
Hark, how He calls the tender lambs,
    And folds them in His arms!

"Permit them to approach," He cries,
    "Nor scorn their humble name;
For 't was to bless such souls as these,
    The Lord of angels came."

We bring them, Lord, in thankful hands,
  And yield them up to Thee;
Joyful that we ourselves are Thine,—
  Thine let our offspring be.

Ye little flock, with pleasure hear;
  Ye children, seek His face;
And fly with transport to receive
  The blessings of His grace.

If orphans they are left behind,
  Thy guardian care we trust:
That care shall heal our bleeding hearts,
  If weeping o'er their dust.

              Philip Doddridge, b. 1702, *d.* 1751.

INDEX OF FIRST LINES.

	PAGE.
Abide with me! fast falls the even tide.—*Henry Francis Lyte.*	76
All hail the power of Jesus' name.—*Rev. Edward Perronet.*	92
All praise to Thee, my God, this night.—*Bishop Thomas Ken.*	65
Amazing grace! (how sweet the sound!)—*John Newton.*	100
As when the weary traveller gains.—*John Newton.*	6
Christ the Lord is risen to-day.—*Charles Wesley.*	18
Christ, whose glory fills the skies.—*Charles Wesley.*	64
Come, Holy Spirit, come.—*Joseph Hart.*	28
Come, let us join our cheerful songs.—*Isaac Watts.*	88
Come, my soul, thy suit prepare.—*John Newton.*	48
Come, O thou Traveller unknown.—*Charles Wesley.*	70
Come, we that love the Lord.—*Isaac Watts.*	32
Commit thou all thy griefs.—*John Wesley.*	78
Father, I know that all my life.—*Anna Lætitia Waring.*	56
Forever with the Lord.—*James Montgomery.*	84
Friend after friend departs.—*James Montgomery.*	87
From Greenland's icy mountains.—*Bishop Reginald Heber.*	27
Glorious things of Thee are spoken.—*John Newton.*	30
God is the refuge of His saints.—*Isaac Watts.*	99
Hail to the Lord's Anointed.—*James Montgomery.*	23
Hark! the herald angels sing.—~~Bishop Reginald Heber~~.	104
How gentle God's commands.—*Philip Doddridge.*	90
How sweet the name of Jesus sounds.—*John Newton.*	12
Jesu, lover of my soul.—*Charles Wesley.*	62
Jesus, cast a look on me.—*John Berridge.*	60

(107)

INDEX OF FIRST LINES.

	PAGE
Jesus, I love Thy charming name.—*Philip Doddridge.*	74
Jesus, I my cross have taken.—*Henry Francis Lyte.*	74
Jesus shall reign where'er the sun.—*Isaac Watts.*	25
Jesus, where'er Thy people meet.—*William Cowper.*	34
Join all the glorious names.—*Isaac Watts.*	20
Just as I am, without one plea.—*Charlotte Elliott.*	89
Let me but hear my Saviour say.—*Isaac Watts.*	15
Love Divine, all loves excelling.—*Charles Wesley.*	94
My faith looks up to Thee.—*Ray Palmer.*	49
My soul, repeat His praise.—*Isaac Watts.*	35
Not all the blood of beasts.—*Isaac Watts.*	10
Oh, help us, Lord!—each hour of need.—*Henry Hart Milman.*	101
O for a heart to praise my God.—*Charles Wesley.*	52
O for a thousand tongues to sing.—*Charles Wesley.*	11
O God of Jacob, by whose hand.—*Philip Doddridge.*	5
One sweetly solemn thought.—*Phœbe Cary.*	8
One there is above all others.—*John Newton.*	95
Our God, our help in ages past.—*Isaac Watts.*	42
Plunged in a gulf of dark despair.—*Isaac Watts.*	16
Prayer is the soul's sincere desire.—*James Montgomery.*	44
Quiet, Lord, my froward heart.—*John Newton.*	59
Rise, my soul, and stretch thy wings.—*Robert Seagrave.*	41
See Israel's gentle Shepherd stands.—*Philip Doddridge.*	105
Sing to the Lord with joyful voice.—*Isaac Watts.*	97
Songs of praise the angels sang.—*James Montgomery.*	85
Sow in the morn thy seed.—*James Montgomery.*	103
Sun of my soul, Thou Saviour dear.—*John Keble.*	67
Sweet is the work, my God, my King.—*Isaac Watts.*	69
The Lord my Shepherd is.—*Isaac Watts.*	61
There is a fountain filled with blood.—*Augustus Montague Toplady.*	7 37
There is a land of pure delight.—*Isaac Watts.*	91
Thy way, not mine, O Lord.—*Horatius Bonar.*	55

INDEX TO FIRST LINES.

	PAGE.
Triumphant Zion! lift thy head.—*Philip Doddridge.*	98
'T is my happiness below.—*William Cowper.*	7
When all Thy mercies, O my God.—*Joseph Addison.*	45
When I survey life's varied scenes.—*Anne Steele.*	53
When I survey the wondrous cross.—*Isaac Watts.*	13
Why do we mourn departing friends.—*Isaac Watts.*	39
Ye servants of the Lord.—*Philip Doddridge.*	31
Your harps ye trembling saints.—*Augustus Montague Toplady.*	81

BIOGRAPHICAL INDEX.

ADDISON, JOSEPH, son of the Rev. Lancelot Addison, Rector of Milston, afterwards Dean of Litchfield; born at Milston rectory, near Amesbury, in Wiltshire, 1 May, 1672; was made Secretary of State, 1717; died 17 June, 1719. His hymns appeared in the Saturday papers of the *Spectator* during 1712.

BERRIDGE, JOHN, son of a wealthy farmer; born at Kingston, Nottinghamshire, 1 March, 1716; became Vicar of Everton, 1755; died 22 January, 1793. His hymns, which were often adaptations of others already in existence, appeared in "Sion's Songs · or Hymns Composed for the Use of them that love and follow the Lord Jesus Christ in Sincerity" (1785).

BONAR, HORATIUS, D. D., son of James Bonar; born at Edinburgh, 19 December, 1808; Minister of the Free Church of Scotland at Kelso, and now at Grange, Edinburgh. His hymns appeared in "Hymns of Faith and Hope," 1st Series, 1857; 2d Series, 1861; 3d Series, 1866.

CARY, PHŒBE, born in Hamilton County, Ohio, in 1825; died at Newport, R. I., 31 July, 1871. Her "Poems and Parodies" were published in 1854.

COWPER, WILLIAM, of the Inner Temple, son of the Rev. John Cowper, D. D., Rector of Berkhampstead, Hertfordshire; born at the Rectory, 15 November, 1731; died at East Dereham, 25 April, 1800. He united with Newton in writing the "Olney Hymns" (1779), to which he contributed 67 out of 340.

BIOGRAPHICAL INDEX.

DODDRIDGE, PHILIP, D. D., son of an oilman in London; born in London, 26 June, 1702; Pastor of the Congregational Church at Northampton, and Principal of the Theological Academy there; died at Lisbon, 26 October, 1751. His hymns were circulated in manuscript during his life, but it was not till 1755 that they were published, 364 in all, as "Hymns Founded on Various Texts in the Holy Scriptures."

HART, JOSEPH, the son of pious parents; born in London, 1712; Minister of the Congregational Church in Jewin Street Chapel, London; died in London, 24 May, 1768. His "Hymns Composed on Various Subjects" appeared in 1759 (second edition, with Supplement, 1762).

HEBER, REGINALD, D. D., son of Reginald Heber, Rector of Malpas, Cheshire; born at Malpas, 21 April, 1783; Bishop of Calcutta, 1823; died at Trichinopoly, 2 April, 1826. His hymns appeared in the *Christian Observer* (1811), "Hymns Written and Adapted to the Weekly Church Service of the Year" (1827), edited by his widow; and were collected (to the number of fifty-seven) in his "Poetical Works" (1842).

KEBLE, JOHN, M. A., son of the Rev. John Keble, Rector of Coln S. Aldwyn, Gloucestershire; born at Fairford, Gloucestershire, 22 April, 1792; Vicar of Hursley; died at Bournemouth, 29 March, 1866. His hymns appeared in the *Christian Year* (1827), "Lyra Apostolica (1836), Lyra Innocentium (1846), Miscellaneous Poems (1857)," etc.

KEN, THOMAS, D. D., son of Thomas Ken, attorney, of Furnival's Inn; born at Little Berkhampstead, of Hertfordshire, July, 1637; Bishop of Bath and Wells, 1685; one of the seven Bishops committed to the Tower, 1688; deprived of his See as a Nonjuror, 1691; died 19 March, 1711, at Longleate. His Morning, Evening, and Midnight Hymns appeared in the edition of his "Manual of Prayers for the Use of the Scholars of Winchester College" (1674), published in 1697.

BIOGRAPHICAL INDEX. 113

LYTE, HENRY FRANCIS, M. A., son of Captain Thomas Lyte; born at Ednam, near Kelso, 1 June, 1793; Perpetual Curate of Lower Brixham, Devonshire; died at Nice, 20 November, 1847. His hymns appeared in "Poems Chiefly Religious" (1833), "Miscellaneous Poems" (1868), and "The Spirit of the Psalms" (1834; 5th edition, corrected and enlarged, 1841).

MILMAN, HENRY HART, D. D., son of Sir Francis Milman, a physician, born in London, 10 February, 1791; Dean of St. Paul's; died at Sunningfield, near Ascot, 24 September, 1868. His hymns appeared in "Hymns adapted to the Weekly Church Service of the Year," edited by Mrs. Heber" (1827); and in "A Selection of Psalms and Hymns for the use of St. Margaret's, Westminster (1837).

MONTGOMERY, JAMES, son of the Rev. John Montgomery, a Moravian Minister settled in Ireland; born at Irvine, in Ayrshire, 4 November, 1771; editor of the *Sheffield Iris;* died at Sheffield, 30 April, 1854. His hymns appeared in "Songs of Zion, being Imitations of [fifty-six of the] Psalms" (1822); "The Christian Psalmist" (1825; 3d edition, 1826); "Original Hymns for Public, Private, and Social Devotion" (1853).

NEWTON, JOHN, son of a sea-captain; born in London, 24 July, 1725; Curate of Olney, Bucks, and afterwards Rector of S. Mary Woolnoth, London; died 21 December, 1807. His hymns appeared in the "Olney Hymns" (1779).

PALMER, RAY, D. D., son of the Hon. Thomas Palmer, Judge in Rhode Island; born at Little Compton, Rhode Island, U. S., 12 November, 1808; Pastor of the Congregational Church at Albany, and now Secretary of the Congregational Union, at New York. His "Hymns and Sacred Pieces" appeared in 1865; and his hymns also appeared in "Lowell Mason's Collection" (1832), and "Hymns of my Holy Hours" (1867).

PERRONET, EDWARD, son of Rev. Vincent Perronet, Vicar of Shoreham · a preacher with the Wesleys, afterwards with Lady

Huntington, then to a small congregation unattached: died January, 1793. His hymns appeared in "Occasional Verses, Moral and Sacred" (1785).

SEAGRAVE, ROBERT, was born at Twyford, Leicestershire, in 1693. He studied at Cambridge, graduated in 1718. In 1739 he was appointed Sunday evening lecturer at Lorimer's Hall, London. He afterwards preached in the Tabernacles in connection with the Calvanistic Methodists. The date of his death is unknown. He published some treatises on doctrinal subjects, and on the duties of the ministry. In 1742 he published "Hymns for Christian Worship. His hymns were published by Sedgwick in 1860.

STEELE, ANNE, daughter of William Steele, a timber merchant, who also ministered to the Baptist Church at Broughton, Hampshire; born at Broughton in 1717; died at Broughton, after a life of suffering, in November, 1778. Her "Poems and Hymns" were published under the assumed name of *Theodosia*, and in 1863 the "Hymns, Psalms, and Poems" previously scattered through many publications, were issued by Mr. Sedgwick in one volume.

TOPLADY, AUGUSTUS MONTAGUE, son of Major Toplady; born at Farnham, Surrey, 4 November, 1740; Vicar of Broad Hembury, Devonshire; died at Knightsbridge, London, 11 August, 1778. His hymns (about a hundred and sixteen) appeared in "Poems on Sacred Subjects" (1759), the "Gospel Magazine" (1770–1776), and elsewhere, and have been re-publishad in a complete edition by Mr. Sedgwick (1860).

WARING, ANNA LÆTITIA, daughter of Elijah Waring; born at Neath, Glamorganshire. Her hymns have appeared in "Hymns and Meditations" by A. L. W. (1850), "Additional Hymns" (1858), and in the *Sunday Magazine* (1871).

WATTS, ISAAC, D. D., son of a schoolmaster at Southampton; born at Southampton, 17 July, 1674; Minister of the Congregational Church at Berry Street, London; has been called the father of English hymnody; died at Stoke Newington, 25 November, 1748. His hymns appeared in "Horæ Lyricæ" (1706); "Hymns and Spiritual Songs" (1707; enlarged edition, 1709); "Divine Songs for Children" (1715); "The Psalms of David imitated in the Language of the New Testament, and applied to the Christian State and Worship" (1719); and appended to his Sermons.

WESLEY, CHARLES, M. A., son of Samuel Wesley, Rector of Epworth, Lincolnshire; born at Epworth, 18 December, 1708; was missionary (in Georgia, U. S.) of the Society for the Propagation of the Gospel; united with his brother John in preaching; became the poet of Methodism; died in London, 29 March, 1788. His hymns (over six thousand) appeared in:—"A Collection of Psalms and Hymns" by John Wesley (1738), "Hymns and Sacred Poems" (1739, 1740, 1742, 1749, 1756), "Hymns on God's Everlasting Love" (1741), "Hymns for the Watch Nights (1744), "Hymns for Times of Trouble and Persecution" (1744, 1745), "Hymns on the Lord's Supper" (1745), "Hymns for the Nativity of Our Lord" (2d ed., 1745, 1772), "Hymns for those that Seek, and those that have Found, Redemption in the Blood of Jesus Christ" (1746), "Hymns for our Lord's Resurrection" (1746,) "Hymns for our Lord's Ascension" (1746), "Hymns for New Year's Day" (1750-1788), Hymns of Intercession for all Mankind" (1758), Funeral Hymns" (1759), "Short Hymns" (two thousand one hundred and forty-five) on Select Passages of the Holy Scriptures" (1762), "Hymns for Children, and Others of Riper Years" (1763).

WESLEY, JOHN, M. A., son of the Rev. Samuel Wesley, Rector of Epworth, Lincolnshire; born at Epworth, 17 June, 1703; Curate at Epworth; afterwards founder of Methodism; died in London, 2 March, 1791. His hymns, which were mostly translations from the German, appeared in his "Collection of Psalms and Hymns," the original (1738), and subsequent editions. He translated twenty nine from the German, two from the French, and one from the Spanish., a language he learned in America.

www.ingramcontent.com/pod-product-compliance
Lightning Source LLC
Chambersburg PA
CBHW020124170426
43199CB00009B/631